© Stonewell Healing Press, 2025
All rights reserved.

This book is a labor of care. Please do not copy, share, or distribute any part of it—digitally or physically—without written permission from the author or publisher, except for brief excerpts used in reviews or critical articles. Your respect helps this work reach others who need it.

This workbook is not a replacement for therapy, crisis support, or mental health treatment. It's meant to offer reflection, comfort, and growth—not clinical care. If you're struggling, please reach out to a licensed professional. You matter too much to go through it alone.

Every effort has been made to ensure this content is accurate, responsible, and thoughtful. The author and publisher cannot guarantee outcomes and are not liable for misuse or misinterpretation of the material.

Thank you for being here. We're honored to walk beside you.

M. Tourangeau
Stonewell Healing Press

TABLE OF CONTENTS

SECTION 1 -   12

What No One Talks About

SECTION 2-   40

This Wasn't Your Fault

SECTION 3 -   68

The Shame Nobody Talks About

SECTION 4 -   94

Relief, Regret, and the Complexity of Grief

SECTION 5 -   116

Rewriting the Story

SECTION 6 -   142

Judgment, Shame, and the Silent Grief

Stonewell Healing Press

TABLE OF CONTENTS

SECTION 7 -   **166**

Relief – The Emotion You're Not Supposed to Feel

SECTION 8-   **186**

The Loneliness of Doing the Right Thing

SECTION 9 -   **210**

Regret, Rumination, and the Loop That Won't Let Go

SECTION 10 -   **230**

Who Am I Now Without Them?

SECTION 11 -   **252**

Rebuilding Trust

CLOSING   **276**

The Paper Trail: Protecting Yourself with Documentation

Stonewell Healing Press

Dedicated to those who had to make the decision that broke their own heart.

STONEWELL HEALING PRESS

HOW TO USE THIS WORKBOOK

Take your time with this. The more you pause to really think about each question and answer honestly, the more space you create for reflection. And with deeper reflection, this experience can open up new understanding and healing you might not expect.

Be honest with yourself—there's no judgment here. This is your private space. If you want, you can even throw this book away or burn it later to keep your secrets safe. That said, be mindful of how much you dive in. Healing and reflection around tough, sensitive topics can bring up strong feelings—and yes, it can get triggering. So here's your gentle trigger warning.

The real progress comes when you practice the skills, not just read about them. The more you try them out in your life, the more helpful this workbook will be.

STONEWELL HEALING PRESS

ASSESSMENT

WHERE AM I NOW?

Before we begin, take a moment to honestly check in with yourself by rating these statements on a scale from 1 (not at all) to 10 (completely):

1-10

1. How aware are you of your feelings about your loss, and how easily can you name them without judgment or suppression?

2. To what extent are you able to treat yourself with understanding and kindness instead of guilt, shame, or self-recrimination?

3. How comfortable are you recognizing that you can feel grief, relief, love, and even conflicting emotions all at the same time?

4. How capable are you of honoring and validating your grief, even when others don't understand, minimize, or dismiss it?

5. To what degree do you trust that your past choices — even painful, morally complex ones — were the most compassionate and responsible you could make?

6. How attuned are you to your body's signals of stress, grief, or relief, and how effectively can you soothe and ground yourself when triggered?

7. How able are you to integrate difficult, morally charged experiences without feeling permanently "damaged" or guilty?

8. How fully can you hold your story — the hopes, the grief, the love, and the limits — as your own, without erasing or minimizing any part of it?

SECTION ONE

What No One Talks About

There are things you can't say out loud. Like how scared you were. Like how angry. Like how the decision didn't feel like a choice, but a corner you were backed into — quietly, over time, until there was nothing else left. You loved your pet. And you also feared them. You loved your pet. And they couldn't be safe. You loved your pet — and now they're gone, and it was you who said yes.

This isn't the kind of grief people want to hear about. It's not clean. It's not tidy. It's grief with blood under its nails. And when it's this complicated, it's easy to feel like you don't deserve to mourn at all.
But you do. You absolutely do. You were there through it all. You made the hardest call a person can make. And you do not have to carry this grief in the dark anymore.

Making Sense Of It
If You're Still Not Sure You Deserve to Grieve

It's so common, in the aftermath of behavioral euthanasia, to circle around the same haunting questions: Could I have tried harder? Was my pet just misunderstood? Did I fail in my role as their protector? Maybe I was the reason they struggled. These thoughts don't make you weak or guilty—they make you human.

What's happening here is your mind's attempt to make sense of something unbearable. Self-blame gives the illusion of control: If it was my fault, then maybe there was something I could have done differently. That illusion can feel safer than facing the raw truth that sometimes love, training, and effort aren't enough to override biology, trauma, or circumstance.

But here's what matters: the part of you that insists you don't deserve to grieve is not your enemy. It's an old survival strategy, trying to protect you from shame, judgment, and rejection. It believes that if you punish yourself first, no one else can. Yet grief does not require you to earn it.

You are allowed to grieve even if your decision wasn't perfect, even if outsiders don't understand, even if your heart is tangled with conflict. Your pain is not proof of failure—it is proof of love. And that love is worthy of mourning. Always.

Making Sense Of It
Disenfranchised Grief & Moral Injury

One of the most painful parts of behavioral euthanasia is that your grief often doesn't feel welcome in the world around you. Society is quick to offer sympathy when a pet dies of old age or illness—but when the reason is behavioral, the silence can be deafening. This is what's called disenfranchised grief: the kind of mourning that isn't socially recognized, validated, or supported. You may feel like you have to keep your story quiet, or that your heartbreak somehow "doesn't count." But the absence of recognition doesn't make your grief any less real.

Layered into this is something even heavier: moral injury. This happens when the actions you were forced to take—actions rooted in necessity, safety, or love—collide with your own moral compass. You never wanted this. You didn't stop loving your pet. But doing what needed to be done may feel like it violated a sacred bond. That rupture can leave you questioning yourself, struggling to trust your own judgment, and feeling fractured in ways that are hard to put into words.

You are not broken for feeling this way. Disenfranchised grief and moral injury are not signs of weakness—they are natural responses to a devastating and complex loss. Your pain deserves a place to be seen, named, and tended to. This workbook exists for exactly that reason: to give language to what feels unspeakable, to hold space for the love beneath the guilt, and to remind you that this kind of grief was never meant to be carried alone.

What were you never allowed to say about your pet's behavior — even to yourself?

Begin by gently naming the things you hid: the way they lunged, scratched, bit, cowered, or growled. The way you flinched. The things that made others uncomfortable. What did you bury because it felt "wrong" to say out loud — and what did it cost you to keep that in?

What were you never allowed to say about your pet's behavior — even to yourself?

When did you start to feel truly alone in this?

Trace the quiet moments that began to isolate you: the vet visit that didn't help, the friend who changed the subject, the post you deleted before finishing. When did the silence start to feel heavier than the fear?

When did you start to feel truly alone in this?

What would you say to someone who had to make this decision — but wasn't you?

Let yourself step out of the storm and speak to another person going through it. What would you say to a stranger who was weeping over their pet, their guilt, and the choice they had to make? Notice the compassion you offer them — and how hard it is to offer it to yourself.

_____
_____
_____
_____
_____
_____
_____
_____
_____
_____
_____
_____

What would you say to someone who had to make this decision — but wasn't you?

What beliefs do you carry about what "loving enough" should look like?

Many of us internalize harmful beliefs about love and sacrifice — that love means never giving up, or that real love could have saved them. Where did those stories come from? Do they still serve you? Could both love and letting go coexist?

What beliefs do you carry about what "loving enough" should look like?

What are you most afraid people would say if they knew the whole story?

This prompt invites radical honesty. Not to re-traumatize, but to acknowledge the shame, judgment, or rejection you may fear. Write out the harshest voices — then pause. Whose voices are they really? Are they true? Are they kind?

What are you most afraid people would say if they knew the whole story?

If your grief had a shape or texture, what would it be?

This is a somatic invitation to describe the felt sense of your grief — heavy? Acidic? Frozen? Numb? Tense? Externalizing it gives it dimension. You don't have to carry it invisibly.

If your grief had a shape or texture, what would it be?

What do you wish had happened instead?

Let yourself explore the version of the story that still lives in your body: where they got better, where you found a miracle solution, where it ended differently. This is not about rewriting reality — it's about honoring the emotional residue of what couldn't be, and giving that grief room to breathe.

What do you wish had happened instead?

TRACING THE TRUTH

THE TRUTH YOU WEREN'T ALLOWED TO TELL

Sometimes the weight of this grief isn't just the loss itself—it's the silence around it. The things you weren't allowed to name, the feelings you swallowed, the truths you've kept locked inside. Holding all of that in your body is exhausting. This exercise gives you permission to finally let those words live somewhere outside of you, without judgment, without editing, without needing anyone else to understand.

Why it helps:
Unspoken truths fester. They lodge themselves in the body as tension, shame, or restlessness. Writing them down gives your nervous system an outlet—your story no longer has to live only inside you. The act of putting it on paper is both a release and a reclamation. It says: this happened, it mattered, and I get to tell it. You don't need to make it neat. You don't need to make it make sense. You only need to let it out.

Title your page: "The truth I wasn't allowed to say out loud…"
Write freely—messy, raw, contradictory. No editing.
Name whatever comes: fear, shame, tenderness, anger, or even nothing. If nothing, write "I don't feel anything" and explore why.
When you're done, close it. Keep it safe or destroy it—whatever feels right.
Aftercare: Drink water. Stretch or shake your hands. Touch something grounding. Tell your body: The truth is spoken. I'm still here.

TRACING THE TRUTH

THE TRUTH YOU WEREN'T ALLOWED TO TELL

TRACING THE TRUTH

THE TRUTH YOU WEREN'T ALLOWED TO TELL

TRACING THE TRUTH

THE TRUTH YOU WEREN'T ALLOWED TO TELL

TRACING THE TRUTH

THE TRUTH YOU WEREN'T ALLOWED TO TELL

EXTERNALIZE THE INNER CRITIC

The inner critic often masquerades as truth, when really it's a protective part gone overboard. By externalizing it — drawing it, collaging it, or writing it as a character — you create distance. Suddenly, it's not you failing; it's a scared or rigid part doing its job too harshly. Research in IFS and narrative therapy shows that putting dialogue on paper softens shame and restores self-leadership. Adding a Wise Friend voice gives you access to compassion and balance. The final boundary statement reminds the critic: its role is protection, not punishment. That's where healing starts.

Create the Critic — Draw, doodle, or collage how your inner critic might look. Don't worry about artistic skill.

Dialogue — Write a short back-and-forth:
You: "I hear you saying I failed."
Critic: "I don't want you to get hurt."
Wise Friend: "You can protect without tearing down."

Set a Boundary — End the dialogue with a firm line: "Your job is protection, not punishment. I'll take it from here."

MAPPING YOUR RESILIENCE

When life is painful, the spotlight lands on what's broken or lost. But every hard season you've lived through also carries evidence of your resilience. Mapping your past with a "strength lens" helps you reclaim those forgotten skills — endurance, creativity, boundary-setting, persistence, humor, or compassion. Trauma research shows that naming and revisiting these strengths rebuilds self-trust. Instead of seeing your past only as a string of wounds, you begin to recognize the ways you showed up for yourself. Circling three core strengths creates a personal toolkit you can consciously bring forward into your next chapter.

1 **Draw Your Timeline** —Mark a few "hard seasons" you've lived through on the timeline.

2 **Name Strengths** — Under each event, write one or two strengths you used to get through (e.g., courage, asking for help, persistence).

3 **Circle Three** — Look at the whole map. Circle three strengths that feel most alive, relevant, or needed for where you're headed now.

4 **Carry Them Forward** — Write them on a sticky note or card where you'll see them often — reminders that you've done hard things before, and you will again.

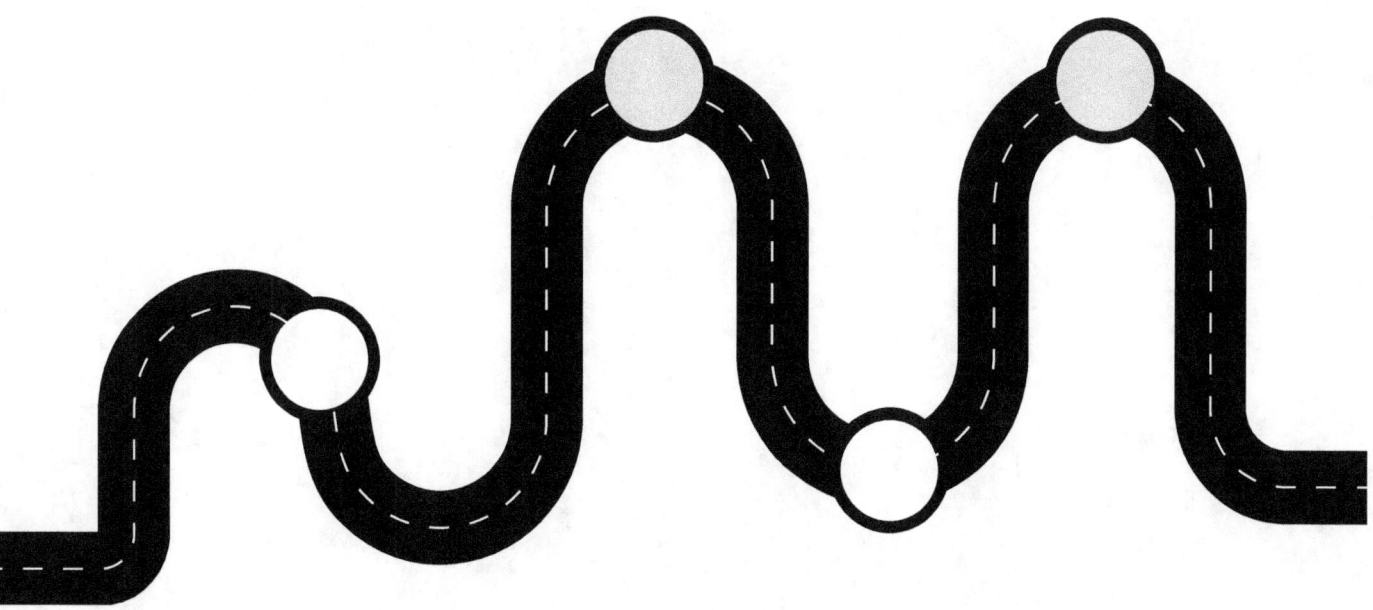

SECTION TWO

This Wasn't Your Fault

Grief is already hard. But grief laced with blame is brutal. It turns inward, eats at your self-worth, and distorts your memory of what really happened. After behavioral euthanasia, that voice gets loud: "You failed them. You gave up. You didn't try hard enough." It asks questions that can never be answered and demands a perfection that no human could have achieved.

You were not meant to carry this story with a scapegoat's weight.
You didn't cause this.
This wasn't your fault.
There's a difference between being responsible for a decision and being to blame for what made the decision necessary. Those are not the same — but trauma confuses them. Survival confuses them. And guilt will lie to keep you stuck.

In this chapter, we gently begin to untangle what was never yours to hold — so your grief can breathe. So your love doesn't have to keep proving itself. So you can begin to come back home to yourself.

Making Sense Of It
Trauma Narratives, Guilt, and the Weight of "Shoulds"

When we're faced with an impossible choice — like ending a pet's life because their behavior became dangerous or unmanageable — the brain doesn't just remember it. It loops it. Over and over, you may find yourself replaying the scene, filling it with "I should have…," "If only I had…," or "Maybe I could have…" That mental spiraling isn't weakness; it's your nervous system's desperate attempt to rewrite a story that felt out of your control.

This is what trauma does: it latches onto unfinished chapters, trying to reorganize them until they make sense. But in situations like behavioral euthanasia, there is no neat ending. The "what ifs" and "should haves" become a way of avoiding the unbearable truth — that you loved deeply and still had to make a choice that went against everything in you.

Many people in this place also wrestle with hyper-responsibility — the ingrained belief that if something went wrong, it must somehow be your fault. It's a common pattern in people who have carried caretaking roles, perfectionism, or unresolved trauma. That voice insists that love means fixing everything, no matter the cost. But that isn't love. That's survival wiring.

The harder truth — and the more healing one — is that you made the most compassionate choice available in an impossible moment. Not the perfect choice (because there wasn't one), but the humane one. Your guilt is not evidence that you failed. It's evidence that you cared enough to hurt this much.

What part of you still believes this was your fault — and what is it afraid would happen if you stopped blaming yourself?

This prompt asks you to meet your inner critic with compassion. Is it afraid of judgment? Of losing the last thread connecting you to your pet? Of being seen as a bad person? Let that voice speak, without letting it take over.

What part of you still believes this was your fault — and what is it afraid would happen if you stopped blaming yourself?

What invisible labor did you do before the end that no one saw?

Write about the vet visits, the second chances, the fear you hid, the tools you tried, the sleepless nights. Name it all. Let yourself be witnessed — even by the page.

What invisible labor did you do before the end that no one saw?

How has guilt shaped the way you remember the ending?

Guilt often edits the story, placing a spotlight on what went wrong and erasing what went right. What details has your guilt magnified or erased? What happens when you widen the lens?

How has guilt shaped the way you remember the ending?

What would it mean to believe you did your best?

Let yourself try on this idea like a coat: that you truly did all you could with what you knew, who you were, and the options available. What emotions rise up when you try to believe that?

What would it mean to believe you did your best?

What are the rules you hold yourself to when it comes to love, protection, and "not giving up"?

List them. Unpack them. Where did they come from — childhood? Culture? Online messaging? What would a more human — not superhuman — version of those rules look like?

What are the rules you hold yourself to when it comes to love, protection, and "not giving up"?

Who benefits when you believe it was your fault?

A confronting question. Does it protect others? Shield professionals who failed you? Let a system off the hook? Keep you from having to feel grief more directly? No blame — just truth.

Who benefits when you believe it was your fault?

Where in your body do you feel the weight of self-blame most?

This somatic prompt invites you to map the physical location of guilt. Does it sit in your chest? Your gut? Your jaw? What does it feel like? What would ease it by even 1%?

Where in your body do you feel the weight of self-blame most?

TRACING THE TRUTH

THE GUILT REWRITE

When guilt takes over, it can feel like there's only one version of what happened – the harsh, punishing one. But stories are never that simple. There's always another perspective, often kinder and closer to the truth. This exercise helps you hold both, so you're not trapped inside guilt's single narrative.

Why it helps:
Writing the story twice – once from guilt and once from compassion – interrupts the loop of self-blame. It gives your mind a new pathway, showing that truth can hold both grief and tenderness. Over time, this practice weakens guilt's grip and strengthens the voice that sees your humanity.

Write guilt's version. Tell the story as your guilt sees it – sharp, unfiltered, accusing. Don't soften it. Get it out of your head and onto the page.
Pause and reset. When you finish, breathe deeply, stretch, or shake out your hands. Signal to your body that round one is done.
Write again with compassion. Now imagine someone who truly loves you was watching it unfold – a friend, therapist, or your future self. Tell the same story with context, care, and truth.
Compare both versions. What's different? What stays the same? Which feels more believable, more liveable?

TRACING THE TRUTH

THE GUILT REWRITE

TRACING THE TRUTH

THE GUILT REWRITE

TRACING THE TRUTH

THE GUILT REWRITE

TRACING THE TRUTH

THE GUILT REWRITE

TRACING THE TRUTH

THE GUILT REWRITE

TRACING THE TRUTH

THE GUILT REWRITE

ACTION

MASK WORK

We all carry layers — the parts we show and the parts we protect. Trauma, stress, or social expectation often make us overinvest in the "front" mask while ignoring the care the "back" side needs. This exercise gives you a safe way to explore both sides without forcing exposure. By naming what's hidden, you acknowledge your needs; by sharing a small sliver with a trusted person, you practice vulnerability and connection without danger. It helps build trust in yourself — that you can both protect and reveal, and that your inner life is valid and worthy of care. Over time, you may notice your outer mask feels lighter, more authentic, because your inner self has space to be seen.

Fill Them In — List words, phrases, or images for each side. Don't censor yourself.

Choose a Safe Reveal — Pick one tiny sliver from the Back mask and plan to share it with a safe person this week.

Reflect — Notice what it feels like to acknowledge and/or reveal that part of yourself.

What the world sees | **What you protect or that needs care**

FEELING IN MOTION

Our bodies carry what words often can't — tension, joy, grief, or relief. Moving intentionally helps you process and release emotions stored in the body, while giving a tangible sense of your day's narrative. Ending in a posture of strength signals to your nervous system: I survived, I'm here, I can hold myself steady. This isn't about dancing perfectly or performing for anyone; it's about giving your inner experience a voice through movement, noticing how small gestures can express complex feelings. Over time, this practice reconnects body and mind, helping you feel grounded, seen, and resilient.

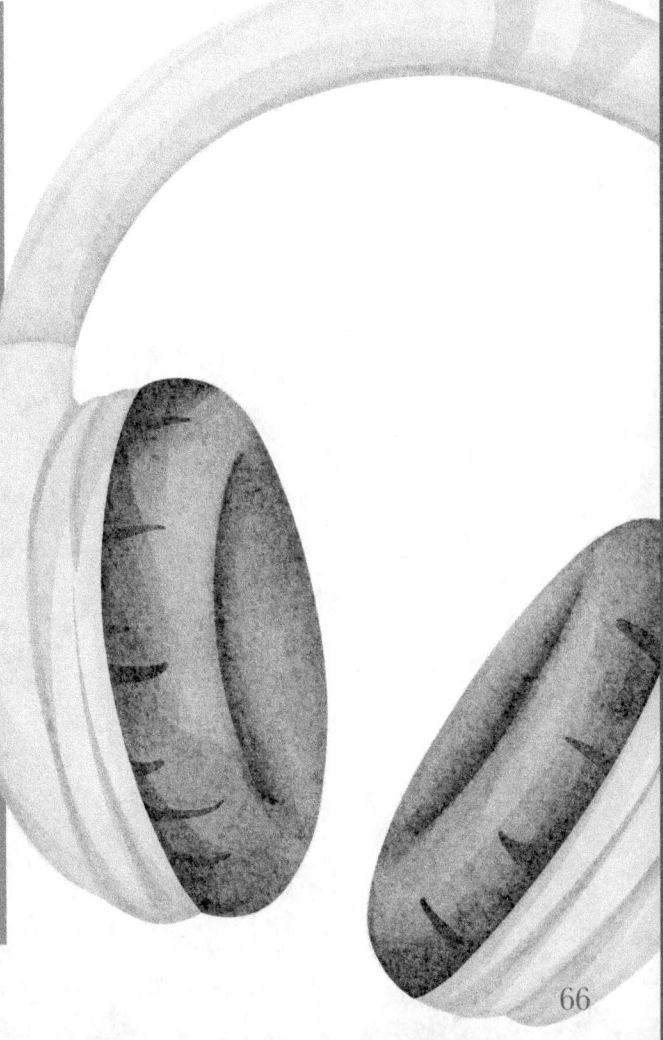

Choose a Song — Something that matches or invites movement for your current state.

Move Freely — Let your body express today's story. Small gestures count — a hand to heart, a sway, a shrug.

Notice — Pay attention to tension, ease, or areas that want attention.

End in Strength — Finish in a posture that conveys groundedness and safety (feet planted, shoulders relaxed, chest open). Hold for 30 seconds.

Reflect — Journal a few words about what your body expressed and how it feels afterward.

SECTION THREE

The Shame Nobody Talks About

Grief is lonely. But grief after behavioral euthanasia is something else entirely. It's a silence so heavy it swallows you. It's knowing people won't get it — or worse, that they'll judge you if they do. You can't post about it. You can't say it out loud without watching people flinch. You're grieving your best friend, while also defending your humanity.
Shame enters here, through the cracks that compassion should have filled. You wonder: "Was I weak? Was I selfish? Did I kill my pet just to make my life easier?" You fear someone will ask what happened, and you won't know how to answer.

This chapter is for that aching place. The one that still hides. The one that thinks this grief is less valid because you were forced to make an impossible call — and others don't understand what it cost you.
Here, we'll name what the world doesn't. And reclaim the right to grieve without apology.

Making Sense Of It
When Silence Becomes a Second Wound

One of the most painful truths about behavioral euthanasia is that the loss rarely exists in isolation. The moment you said goodbye was devastating enough — but then came the silence. Friends didn't know what to say. Family members avoided the subject. Some people gave quick, dismissive comments: "Well, at least you tried" or "That's what happens with dogs like that." Instead of being met with open arms and empathy, you were met with hesitation, judgment, or nothing at all. That absence of compassion carves its own wound — a wound called shame.

Shame isn't just about guilt; it's about identity. It whispers, "You must be a bad person if others can't even look at your pain." In trauma recovery, we see this often: when empathy is missing, shame fills the void. You begin to believe that your grief is somehow illegitimate, that your loss "doesn't count" the way it would if your pet had died from old age or illness. This is disenfranchised grief — grief that society fails to recognize as valid.

The silence doesn't just sting emotionally; it works its way into the body. It shows up as heaviness in your chest, tension in your stomach, restlessness at night. Your nervous system interprets the lack of support as danger, reinforcing a loop of isolation and self-blame. And if you already carry traits of hyper-responsibility, perfectionism, or past trauma, the shame hits even harder. You start replaying moments, questioning yourself, rewriting history in a desperate attempt to find the version where you could have prevented the unpreventable.

What parts of your story do you feel like you have to hide from others?

Are there details you leave out when explaining what happened? What words feel too "ugly," too complicated, or too easily misinterpreted? What would it feel like to tell the whole story?

What parts of your story do you feel like you have to hide from others?

Where do you feel shame in your body? And when did it start?

Shame is physical. It crouches in the chest, burns in the throat, tightens in the belly. Try to trace its earliest memory — was it the decision itself? Someone's reaction? A specific moment after?

Where do you feel shame in your body? And when did it start?

What would you say to someone else who made the exact same choice?

If your best friend had to put down their pet due to behavior beyond help — how would you speak to them? What tone would you use? How does that compare to how you speak to yourself?

What would you say to someone else who made the exact same choice?

What messages (from culture, internet, or pet communities) have shaped your shame?

Have you seen posts that say, "There's no such thing as a bad pet, only bad owners"? Have you absorbed messages that suggest love can always fix behavior? Write down the beliefs you've internalized — and challenge them.

What messages (from culture, internet, or pet communities) have shaped your shame?

What are you afraid people would think if they knew the truth?

Finish this sentence: "If people knew I euthanized my pet for behavioral reasons, they would think I'm..." Let the fear speak honestly. Then explore whether it's true — or whether it's trauma talking.

What are you afraid people would think if they knew the truth?

What is the difference between guilt and shame — and which one are you really feeling?

Guilt says, "I did something bad." Shame says, "I am bad." Explore where you are on that spectrum. Can you name the emotions more precisely?

What is the difference between guilt and shame — and which one are you really feeling?

What parts of your love were invisible to outsiders?

The quiet protection. The vigilance. The grief that began long before the ending. Write about what no one else saw — but you'll never forget.

What parts of your love were invisible to outsiders?

TRACING THE TRUTH

LETTERS TO THE WORLD

Grief becomes heavier when the world doesn't see it. This exercise gives your pain a voice — both the fury at misunderstanding and the compassion you need from yourself. It's a structured way to honor what happened, release judgment, and reclaim your own narrative.

Why it helps:
Writing to the world externalizes frustration, judgment, and disenfranchised grief — giving it shape and containment. Writing to yourself internalizes validation, compassion, and perspective. Together, these letters create a bridge between what was denied to you and the acknowledgment your mind and body need to heal. This practice rewires self-criticism into self-compassion and helps reclaim authority over your own story.

Letter to the World: Begin a letter addressed to society, your friends, your vet, or anyone who didn't understand. Let it be raw, messy, angry, and honest. Write what you've wanted to scream: the judgment, the abandonment, the misunderstandings. Don't edit, don't soften — let it all out.
Pause and Ground: Take a few deep breaths. Shake out your hands. Acknowledge the energy you've released.
Letter to Yourself: Now write a second letter — this time to you, from the version of yourself that witnessed the entire struggle. Speak with empathy, seeing your efforts, your impossibly hard choices, and your love. Offer the words you needed most in that moment.

TRACING THE TRUTH

LETTERS TO THE WORLD

TRACING THE TRUTH

LETTERS TO THE WORLD

TRACING THE TRUTH

LETTERS TO THE WORLD

TRACING THE TRUTH

LETTERS TO THE WORLD

SELF-COMPASSION BREAK

When stress, shame, or pain flare up, most of us go straight into self-criticism: Why can't I handle this better? What's wrong with me? That inner attack only tightens the spiral. Kristin Neff's Self-Compassion Break interrupts that cycle. It gives you three small handholds: recognition of your pain, the reminder you're not alone in it, and an active choice to soften instead of harden against yourself. With repetition, your nervous system learns that you don't have to white-knuckle through suffering or numb out — you can meet yourself with the same tenderness you'd extend to a friend. That shift doesn't erase the pain, but it changes the way it lands in your body. Over time, it builds resilience, because you're no longer abandoned in hard moments; you become your own safe ally.

Notice —
Pause and acknowledge: "This is hard. This hurts."

Common Humanity —
Say: "Others feel this too. I'm not the only one struggling."

Kindness —
Place a hand on your chest or cheek and whisper: "May I be gentle with myself right now."

POCKET MOOD LIFTERS

When life feels heavy, it's easy to forget what actually helps. In hard moments, the brain tends to focus on what's wrong, not what's available. An Antidote List is your preloaded reminder: ten small, proven things that shift your state even a little. These aren't grand fixes or instant cures — they're micro-adjustments that keep you from sliding deeper into the stuckness. Pairing an antidote before a hard task helps you face it with steadier energy; using one after provides recovery and closure so you don't carry the weight forward. Over time, this list becomes muscle memory — your nervous system learns, When I struggle, I have options. That's the opposite of hopelessness.

1 **List Ten** — Write down 10 things that reliably lift your mood (a song, a walk, fresh air, texting a safe friend, lighting a candle). Keep them small and doable.

....

....

....

....

....

....

....

2 **Use Before** — Pick one before facing a task you tend to dread. Let it soften resistance.

3 **Use After** — Choose another as a closing ritual. Let it tell your body, That part is done. I'm safe again.

SECTION FOUR

Relief, Regret, and the Complexity of Grief

There's a moment, sometimes days or hours after the euthanasia, where the house is still. Where you expect chaos — and it doesn't come. You don't have to worry anymore. No more safety plans. No more walking on eggshells. No more dread in your chest when a sound startles them. You breathe. And that breath feels like betrayal.
This is the heartbreak of relief.

It's the place where trauma and grief collide in confusing, contradictory ways. You feel peace. You feel guilt. You feel like a monster for even noticing the quiet feels good. But this part of grief is just as real as the sadness. It's your nervous system, softening after months or years of being on high alert. That softening does not mean you didn't love them. It means you did the hard thing. The thing that cost you everything.
Let's step into this complexity — gently. Let's hold space for the grief that doesn't look like grief.

Making Sense Of It
Dual Process Model & Nervous System Relief

Grief isn't a straight line — it's a landscape of contradictions, loops, and unexpected emotional shifts. The Dual Process Model of bereavement describes two intertwined modes: loss-oriented coping, where you feel sorrow, heartache, and longing; and restoration-oriented coping, where the mind and body temporarily turn toward relief, distraction, or even numbness. Both are necessary for navigating the full spectrum of loss.

When grief intersects with prolonged trauma caregiving — managing a pet's aggression, safety protocols, or constant vigilance — the emotional aftermath is more complex. Your nervous system was in hypervigilance, a biologically normal trauma response, always scanning for danger. When the stressor ends, your body naturally exhaled, sometimes in the form of relief, lightness, or even quiet joy. This doesn't mean your love was absent. It means your system, which had been in overdrive, finally got a chance to rest.

Regret and guilt often arrive alongside relief. The mind seeks to reconcile "I feel relief" with "I should feel only sadness." Understanding this requires recognizing cognitive dissonance and trauma-informed grief patterns: your emotional experience is valid, even if contradictory. Relief doesn't cancel love, care, or loss — it simply signals that your body and mind are rebalancing.

In this chapter, we explore how to sit with these contradictions tenderly. You will learn strategies to honor your sorrow while acknowledging relief, to validate both guilt and self-compassion, and to recognize that healing doesn't erase grief — it weaves it into a broader, human experience of love, care, and loss. You are not broken. You are navigating the aftermath of an impossible responsibility with courage, tenderness, and resilience.

What does relief look like for you right now — and what does it make you feel?

Has your sleep changed? Are your routines easier? What do you notice about your body or home? Explore how your environment and emotions have shifted — and what feelings that brings up.

What does relief look like for you right now — and what does it make you feel?

Where does guilt show up in your moments of calm?

When you feel okay, what thoughts creep in? Do you tell yourself you should be more devastated? That you should be punished for being at peace? Write about the inner conflict.

Where does guilt show up in your moments of calm?

What was your body carrying, all those weeks or months before the end?

Name the labor of loving a pet who was suffering. The alertness. The anxiety. The helplessness. What did you hold that others never saw?

What was your body carrying, all those weeks or months before the end?

What do you wish someone would say to you — without qualifiers?

Finish the sentence: "I wish someone would just say…" without adding a "but." Let yourself feel what full compassion might sound like.

> What do you wish someone would say to you — without qualifiers?

What do you regret — and what do you know you had no control over?

Separate what you could have done differently from what was never in your hands. Let the complexity have space, but also seek clarity. You don't need to carry blame that isn't yours.

What do you regret — and what do you know you had no control over?

What has this experience taught you about love in its most painful form?

Reflect on how loving them — even in their most unwell moments — shaped you. How did it stretch you, test you, change you?

What has this experience taught you about love in its most painful form?

TRACING THE TRUTH

MAPPING THE MESSY TRUTH OF YOUR EMOTIONS

After caregiving through prolonged stress, grief rarely arrives in tidy, linear packages. Relief can coexist with sorrow, guilt can live alongside tenderness, and numbness might brush up against peace. This exercise gives you explicit permission to notice and name every feeling — even the ones that seem contradictory or "wrong." It's about witnessing your inner reality without judgment.

Why it helps:
Your nervous system needs acknowledgment, not judgment. By visually mapping emotions, you externalize the inner chaos and gain clarity about what each feeling is communicating. This allows you to honor both grief and relief, guilt and tenderness — reducing internalized shame, easing cognitive overload, and reinforcing that contradictory emotions are not moral failings but part of being human.

From the circle, draw lines radiating outward, like a sunburst. At the end of each line, write one emotion you're currently feeling. Examples — relief, grief, guilt, peace, confusion, even numbness.
Under each emotion, write:
- A recent moment, thought, or memory that triggered it
- What this feeling might be trying to protect you from or communicate

When you've completed your sunburst, write at the bottom of the page in bold:
- "I can feel more than one thing. And none of it makes me a bad person."

Sit with the page. Take a deep breath. Let your body register that each emotion has been seen and named.

TRACING THE TRUTH

MAPPING THE MESSY TRUTH OF YOUR EMOTIONS

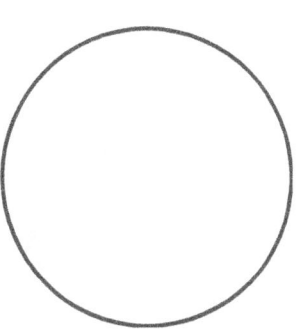

TINY WINS PROTOCOL

When you're overwhelmed, your brain can trick you into believing nothing is possible. Big goals feel impossible, so you stall. But tiny actions build proof: I can move. Completing a single small task sparks dopamine — the brain's reward chemical — and that fuels momentum. Instead of waiting for motivation, you create it by acting first. Two-minute wins keep you out of the freeze state and remind you that forward movement doesn't need to be dramatic to matter. Over time, stacking these little completions can shift your entire day — and even your sense of self. It's not about doing everything; it's about proving to yourself that you can do something.

Pick a micro-task: Something that takes under 2 minutes (wash mug, text back, stretch, shower).

02 Countdown launch: Mental health awareness helps reduce stigma, promotes empathy, and encourages open conversations about mental health concerns.

03 Complete & log: Write it down or check it off for a small hit of satisfaction.

04 Notice momentum: Let the success energy carry you into the next doable action.

05 Repeat daily: Build trust with yourself through small, steady proof points.

ACTION

THREE PILLARS BEFORE NOON

When you're caught in anxiety, depression, or burnout, your nervous system can swing between shutdown and overdrive. The quickest way to steady yourself is to touch three key areas: body, mind, and pleasure. Moving your body brings energy online; completing a mastery task (even something small like an email) restores a sense of competence; and engaging in pleasure reminds you that joy and safety are still accessible. This "trio" isn't about being productive — it's about balance. Think of it as a daily reset button. By noon, if you've already touched your body, completed one mastery task, and tasted one moment of pleasure, you've laid down anchors for resilience. Instead of asking your day to be perfect, you give yourself three touchpoints that prove: I can show up, I can accomplish, and I can enjoy.

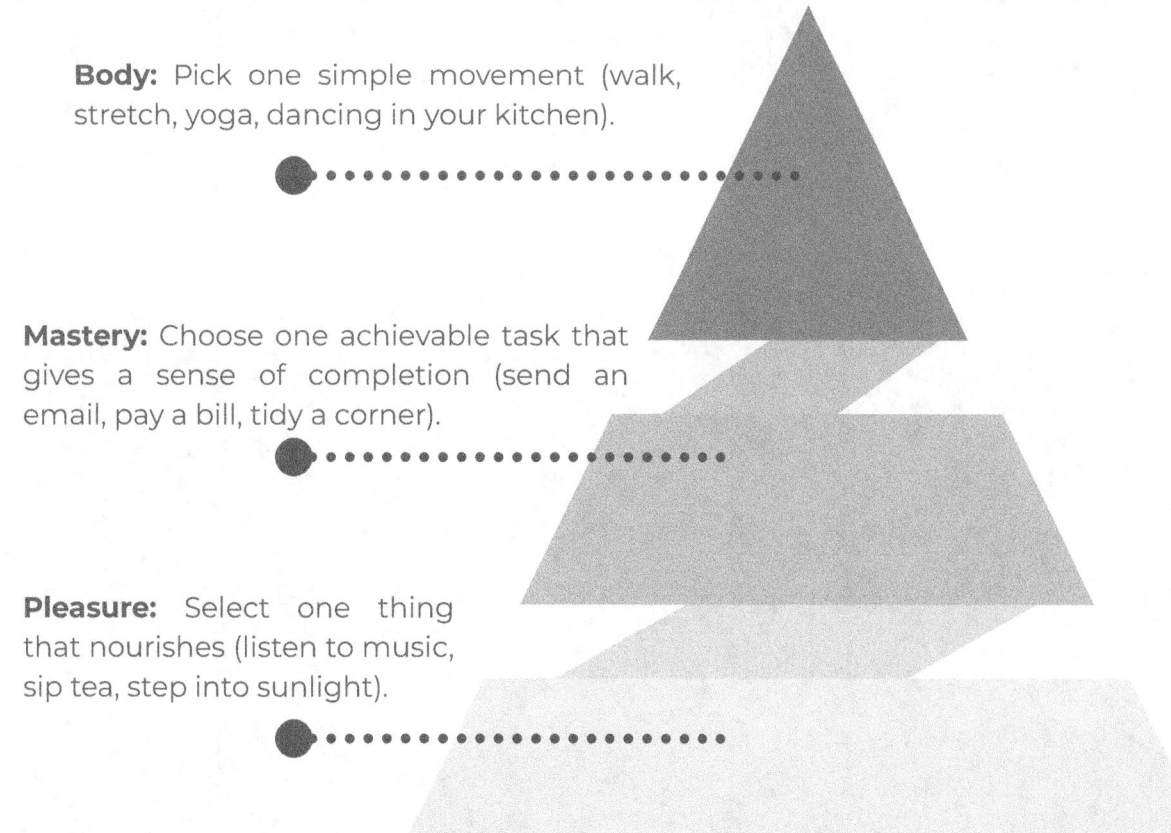

Body: Pick one simple movement (walk, stretch, yoga, dancing in your kitchen).

Mastery: Choose one achievable task that gives a sense of completion (send an email, pay a bill, tidy a corner).

Pleasure: Select one thing that nourishes (listen to music, sip tea, step into sunlight).

Stack them early: Aim to complete all three before noon to set your rhythm.

Reflect briefly: Notice how touching all three domains shifts your mood and energy.

SECTION FIVE

Rewriting the Story

You didn't want this to be the story. Maybe you pictured growing old together, watching your pet mellow with age, finally able to rest in your lap. You thought you had more time. Or you tried everything — medication, specialists, behaviorists — and still, the ending came too soon. Too violently. Too far from love.

This is the grief of what didn't happen. It's not just mourning their death. It's mourning the version of the story you fought for but didn't get.

Grief after behavioral euthanasia is never just one story. It's the real ending, the imagined one, and the dozen alternate realities your brain replays at 3 a.m. It's not about "moving on." It's about learning to hold the heartbreak of what couldn't be — without letting it erase what was.

Making Sense Of It
From Chaos to Compassion

When trauma strikes, it doesn't just wound us emotionally — it interrupts the way our minds naturally make sense of events. Psychologists call this narrative disruption: the experience feels like a story ripped in half, leaving fragments that no longer fit together. With behavioral euthanasia, this disruption can be especially jarring. The ending may feel like a personal failure, a violation of your moral code, or a betrayal of everything you hoped for. Your mind instinctively replays "what ifs," "if onlys," and "should haves," trying to regain control over a situation that was never fully controllable.

Anthropologically, humans have always relied on stories to make meaning of loss — rituals, oral histories, and shared narratives helped communities process grief and trauma. When our grief is unacknowledged or socially silenced, as it often is with morally complex losses, that natural meaning-making process can be blocked. You may feel isolated, confused, or mistrustful of your own memory and judgment.

Meaning reconstruction is the psychological process that helps repair this disruption. It allows you to:
- Grieve the lost narrative — the hopes, dreams, or expectations that the loss shattered
- Integrate the actual ending — acknowledging what happened without erasing the pain
- Reclaim your identity as a compassionate caregiver — honoring the choices you made under impossible conditions

This isn't about pretending everything was fine or forcing closure. It's about sitting with complexity, honoring contradiction, and embracing compassion for yourself. Your story still matters.

What story did you imagine for the two of you — before things got hard?

Write the version you longed for. The ending you thought you'd have. Be as vivid and emotional as you need. Let yourself name the version of life you're grieving.

What story did you imagine for the two of you — before things got hard?

What parts of your actual story still held beauty?

Even amidst the fear, the confusion, the pain — were there moments of connection? Tiny mercies? Write about anything that felt like love, even in the shadows.

What parts of your actual story still held beauty?

What does your brain replay on loop — and what might it be trying to protect?

Are there specific moments, images, or regrets that won't leave you alone? Instead of resisting them, try to listen. What are they trying to resolve, explain, or undo?

What does your brain replay on loop — and what might it be trying to protect?

How have others tried to edit or silence your story?

Have you felt judged, dismissed, or misunderstood? What parts of your truth do you wish you could say without interruption?

How have others tried to edit or silence your story?

What if your story was still a love story — just a brutal, complicated one?

Let yourself write a few sentences beginning with:
"Even though it ended this way..." or
"This was still love, because..."

What if your story was still a love story — just a brutal, complicated one?

What would justice, peace, or redemption look like — even a little?

What do you wish could happen now? Not to rewrite the past, but to give your story a softer landing. Don't limit yourself to what's "realistic." Let your heart speak.

What would justice, peace, or redemption look like — even a little?

What would justice, peace, or redemption look like — even a little?

TRACING THE TRUTH

REWRITING YOUR STORY

When a loss is complex, morally painful, or socially misunderstood, the story you imagined often gets lost somewhere between hope and heartbreak. This exercise invites you to give each version of your story its own space: the life you hoped for, the reality that unfolded, and the meaning you carry forward. You don't have to fix, judge, or make it neat — just witness it, honor it, and integrate it with compassion.

Why it helps:
Some losses leave your heart and your story fractured. This exercise gives each part of your grief its own space: the life you hoped for, the reality you lived, and the meaning you carry forward. You don't have to fix it — just witness, honor, and integrate it.

Step 1 – The Story You Lost

Title this page: "What I Thought It Would Be"

Write out the life you imagined with them. Let yourself mourn the fantasy — the moments, the milestones, the small joys you dreamed of. This is grief, and it's real. Don't censor yourself. Don't rush. Let the longing, sadness, and tenderness flow onto the page.

TRACING THE TRUTH

REWRITING YOUR STORY

Step 2 – The Story That Happened

Title this page: "What Actually Happened"

Now, tell the true story – the messy, painful, honest one. Include the fear, the attempts, the love, and the heartbreak. Don't worry about being the hero. Don't polish it or justify it. Simply witness the reality of what you lived, with all its complexity.

Step 3 – The Story You Choose to Carry Forward

Title this page: "What This Means to Me Now"

Here is where you find your bridge. Reflect on what this story says about your love, your courage, your limits, and your humanity. You're not rewriting the past – you're reclaiming your place within it. This page is your declaration of meaning, integration, and self-compassion.

TRACING THE TRUTH

REWRITING YOUR STORY

STEP: _____

TRACING THE TRUTH

REWRITING YOUR STORY

STEP: _____

TRACING THE TRUTH

REWRITING YOUR STORY

STEP: _____

TRACING THE TRUTH

REWRITING YOUR STORY

STEP: _____

POCKET OF SAFETY

We all carry different "parts" inside us — the critic that nitpicks, the scared kid who panics, the protector who tries to shield us (sometimes harshly). These parts aren't problems; they're survival strategies that formed along the way. The trouble comes when they take over without our awareness. By pausing to check in, you shift into your core Self — the steady, adult "you" who can listen and lead with compassion. This practice doesn't banish the parts; it respects them, thanks them for trying, and gently reminds them they don't have to run the whole show. Over time, this builds more internal harmony and less inner chaos.

Pause and ask
"Who's up right now?" Notice if it's a critic, a scared kid, or a protector energy.

Acknowledge with gratitude
Silently thank this part for its effort to keep you safe or in control.

Close the loop
Let the part know you'll keep checking in, so it doesn't have to hold everything alone.

Ask what it needs
Gently invite the part to share what would help it feel supported today.

Step into Self
From your grounded, adult Self, offer a doable promise — a breath, a boundary, a rest.

YOUR INNER REFUGE

When your nervous system is flooded, your body doesn't always register that the danger has passed. A safe place image gives your brain and body a shortcut to safety — a place it can return to over and over, no matter what's happening outside. By layering in sensory detail (color, sound, scent, texture), you build a vivid "neural anchor" that your system can latch onto when stress spikes. Over time, practicing this not only calms you in the moment but also strengthens your ability to self-soothe. Think of it as a portable sanctuary you carry inside you, available whenever life feels too sharp or overwhelming.

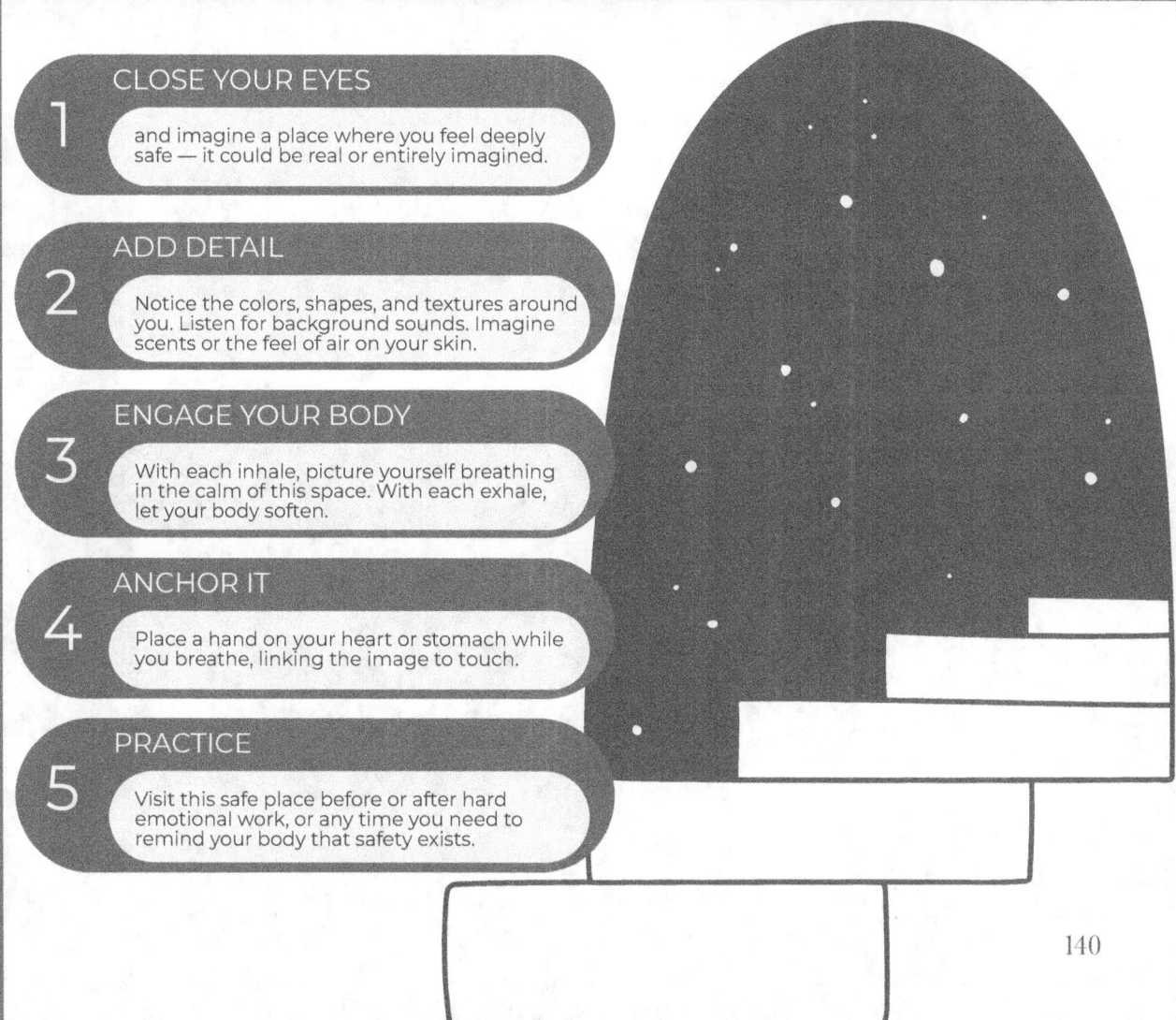

1. CLOSE YOUR EYES
and imagine a place where you feel deeply safe — it could be real or entirely imagined.

2. ADD DETAIL
Notice the colors, shapes, and textures around you. Listen for background sounds. Imagine scents or the feel of air on your skin.

3. ENGAGE YOUR BODY
With each inhale, picture yourself breathing in the calm of this space. With each exhale, let your body soften.

4. ANCHOR IT
Place a hand on your heart or stomach while you breathe, linking the image to touch.

5. PRACTICE
Visit this safe place before or after hard emotional work, or any time you need to remind your body that safety exists.

SECTION SIX

Judgment, Shame, and the Silent Grief

There are kinds of grief you can speak aloud, and kinds you're forced to carry in silence. Behavioral euthanasia often belongs to the second category.

People don't understand. They ask invasive questions. They wonder why you didn't "just try harder" or "find them a farm." Some say nothing at all, sensing something dark and choosing to look away. Their discomfort wraps around your pain like fog — and suddenly, you begin to question yourself too.

This is not just grief. This is shame. And shame thrives in silence. It tells you that what happened was your fault, that you were cruel, weak, or broken for making an impossible decision.

You are not. You did not. This chapter is here to say what the world didn't: You are still allowed to grieve. Your loss is still real. And the pain you feel is a measure of how much you loved.

Making Sense Of It
The Weight of Hidden Shame

Some grief goes unrecognized. In trauma therapy, we call this disenfranchised grief — mourning that isn't publicly acknowledged, supported, or validated. Losing a pet to behavioral euthanasia often falls squarely into this category. Friends, family, or even professionals may avoid the topic, minimize your pain, or silently judge your choices. That lack of acknowledgment isn't just hurtful; it sends a subtle but powerful message that your loss doesn't matter.

When grief is met with silence or misunderstanding, it often turns inward, creating internalized shame. Unlike guilt, which focuses on actions ("I did something wrong"), shame targets the self: "I am something wrong." This is a protective but insidious response — your mind tries to reconcile the unbearable truth by convincing you that your identity itself is flawed.

Anthropologically and psychologically, humans are wired to seek social validation for grief. When that validation is absent, it intensifies isolation and prolongs suffering. Healing begins when you bring this shame into the light: name your feelings, challenge the stories you've inherited about "right" and "wrong," and reconnect with your own inner wisdom.

You are not a monster. You are not alone. Your grief is real. Your choices were human, compassionate, and made in impossible circumstances. The pain you feel is valid — and so are you.

What have you not felt safe to say out loud — even to people who care about you?

Write without censoring. What truths about this experience have felt too messy, dark, or "unacceptable" to speak?

_____
_____
_____
_____
_____
_____
_____
_____
_____
_____
_____
_____
_____

What have you not felt safe to say out loud — even to people who care about you?

What assumptions have people made about your decision — and how have those impacted you?

Even subtle judgments can leave deep wounds. Use this space to unpack how others' words (or silence) affected your grief.

What assumptions have people made about your decision — and how have those impacted you?

What messages have you internalized about what a "good" pet guardian should do?

List the rules, expectations, and beliefs — even unrealistic ones. Where did these come from? Which ones hurt more than they help?

What messages have you internalized about what a "good" pet guardian should do?

If shame had a voice, what would it say? If compassion had a voice, what would it say back?

Write this like a dialogue between two inner parts. Let shame speak honestly — then let compassion respond with truth.

If shame had a voice, what would it say? If compassion had a voice, what would it say back?

Who would you be if you believed your grief deserved to be honored?

Let yourself imagine a version of you who didn't feel the need to hide. What might change in your body, your story, your healing?

Who would you be if you believed your grief deserved to be honored?

What would it feel like to be innocent again — not of wrongdoing, but of blame?

This is deep work. Write into the idea of being human, flawed, loving, and trying — and still worthy of kindness.

What would it feel like to be innocent again — not of wrongdoing, but of blame?

TRACING THE TRUTH

SHAME UNSPOOLING LETTER

Shame thrives in silence. It whispers, repeats, and convinces you that your grief is illegitimate. This exercise gives it a voice – and then allows your compassionate self to respond. By externalizing shame, you start to disentangle it from your identity and reclaim your grief as valid.

Why it helps:
Giving shame a form makes it tangible and less overwhelming. Responding from your kindest self creates a corrective experience, helping your nervous system and mind recognize safety, compassion, and truth.

Give shame a character – Imagine your shame as a person, a shadow, or even a creature. How does it look? How does it speak? Name it.
Write a letter from Shame to you – Let it say everything it's been thinking: "You failed," "You shouldn't feel this," "You could have done more." No filters. Bring it all into the light.
Respond from your wise, compassionate self – This is the part of you that remembers your care, your efforts, your love, and the impossible circumstances. Speak truth, not excuses.
Read the letters aloud or silently – Notice bodily reactions: tension, tears, relief. Let the sensations move.
Optional symbolic release – Tear, burn, or fold Shame's letter. Let your body feel the unspooling of its grip.

TRACING THE TRUTH

SHAME UNSPOOLING LETTER

TRACING THE TRUTH

SHAME UNSPOOLING LETTER

TRACING THE TRUTH

SHAME UNSPOOLING LETTER

TRACING THE TRUTH

SHAME UNSPOOLING LETTER

LESSONS IN INK

After hardship, the brain often circles around the why — why it happened, why you stayed, why you're still hurting. Meaning-making is a way to gently reclaim authorship. By naming what you survived and drawing out what it taught you about your own values and limits, you shift from being swallowed by the story to becoming the narrator of it. This process isn't about silver linings or forced positivity. It's about grounding your pain in context — saying, this mattered, this shaped me, and here's what I'm carrying forward. Closing with a boundary sets a line in the sand: you're not just reflecting on what happened, you're deciding how it changes the way you'll protect yourself in the future.

Headline: Write a short, bold line that sums up what you survived (as if it were on the front page of your personal newspaper).

Lessons: List 3–5 things it revealed about your needs, your limits, or your values.

Boundary: Write one clear, non-negotiable boundary you'll honor from now on.

ACTION

HOLDING HARD DATES

When difficult anniversaries come around—whether it's the day everything fell apart, a loss, or a traumatic turning point—the body remembers even when the mind tries not to. This can show up as anxiety, fatigue, irritability, or old grief bubbling back. Creating an intentional ritual allows you to meet those days with structure instead of being blindsided. By noting the date ahead of time, building in gentle scaffolding (like a support person, a nourishing activity, and less demand on yourself), you create a container for your nervous system. Closing the day with gratitude is not about being thankful for the pain itself, but for your endurance—that you lived through it, and you're still here. Ritual turns an overwhelming anniversary into a moment of honoring resilience.

Mark the Date
Note the anniversary on your calendar so it doesn't sneak up.

Plan Support
Choose one person you can reach out to if things feel heavy.

Nourish
Schedule at least one grounding or soothing activity (walk, bath, journaling, cozy meal).

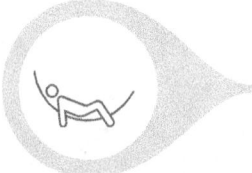
Lighten the Load
Keep your to-do list small that day.

Close with Gratitude
End the evening by writing or saying one thing you're grateful for in your survival.

SECTION SEVEN

Relief — The Emotion You're Not Supposed to Feel

No one tells you how complicated it can be — that you can feel love and devastation and relief in the same breath. That you might cry until your chest aches, and still feel a part of you exhale because the crisis is over.

Maybe the days before were unbearable — locked doors, unpredictable triggers, panic attacks every time the mail arrived. Maybe your pet's suffering had stretched too long. Maybe your nervous system was frayed from holding it all together. And maybe, after it ended, something in your body finally softened. Maybe you slept.

Relief doesn't mean you didn't love them. It doesn't mean you wanted this. It means you're human. It means your body, heart, and soul were carrying too much for too long — and now, something has been released. In this section, we'll name relief without shame. We'll let it coexist with grief, instead of pretending it doesn't belong.

Making Sense Of It
Emotional Simultaneity: Holding Conflicting Feelings

In trauma-informed care, we understand that the human nervous system and psyche are rarely linear. Emotional simultaneity is the concept that you can hold multiple, even contradictory, feelings at the same time — heartbreak and relief, grief and release, sorrow and gratitude. Your mind and body are wired to process trauma in layers, and each emotion is telling you something important about your experience.

After behavioral euthanasia, this is especially pronounced. For weeks, months, or even years, your body may have been locked in hypervigilance — anticipating aggression, escapes, or emergencies. Cortisol levels stayed high. Your nervous system was on high alert. When the immediate threat disappears — even through a choice as devastating as euthanasia — your system can finally exhale. That relief is not betrayal. It's your biology catching up, a physiological signal that the danger has passed.

The challenge is the moral overlay we place on that relief. "I shouldn't feel this. It means I didn't love them enough." That inner dialogue deepens grief unnecessarily. Emotional simultaneity teaches us that we can hold the full truth at once:
- I loved them fiercely.
- I am heartbroken beyond words.
- And yes, I feel relief, exhaustion lifting, a weight gone.

Each feeling has meaning. Each is valid. Healing comes when we let them coexist without judgment, honoring your grief while allowing your body and mind to rest. None of these emotions cancel the others out — they are the human response to impossible circumstances.

In what ways did your life feel unsustainable before your pet passed?

Name what was actually happening — the vigilance, the fear, the limitations. Get honest about what was costing you, emotionally and physically.

In what ways did your life feel unsustainable before your pet passed?

What has changed since their passing — in your body, your routines, or your breath?

Have you noticed moments of calm? Fewer triggers? More freedom? Explore the physical truth, not the moralized one.

What has changed since their passing — in your body, your routines, or your breath?

What messages (internal or external) make you question or judge your relief?

What voices tell you that relief means you're cold, selfish, or unworthy? Where did those ideas come from — and do they serve your healing?

What messages (internal or external) make you question or judge your relief?

What is the difference between being glad it's over, and being glad they're gone?

Explore this distinction with tenderness. Let the nuance live — not everything has to be tidy.

What is the difference between being glad it's over, and being glad they're gone?

What might it feel like to let your body feel relief, without needing to defend or justify it?

Imagine giving yourself permission to fully exhale. What resistance comes up? What softening?

> What might it feel like to let your body feel relief, without needing to defend or justify it?

TRACING THE TRUTH

MAPPING CONFLICTING EMOTIONS

When grief and relief coexist, it can feel confusing – like your heart and body are speaking different languages. This exercise helps you name each emotion, explore what it's trying to tell you, and validate the totality of your experience. You can return to this whenever conflicting feelings arise.

Why it helps:
Unspoken truths fester. They lodge themselves in the body as tension, shame, or restlessness. Writing them down gives your nervous system an outlet—your story no longer has to live only inside you. The act of putting it on paper is both a release and a reclamation. It says: this happened, it mattered, and I get to tell it. You don't need to make it neat. You don't need to make it make sense. You only need to let it out.

Fill out the table on the next page.
- **In the Emotion column,** write each feeling you notice – even if it feels contradictory. Examples: grief, relief, guilt, tenderness, exhaustion.
- **In the Body Sensations / Physical Experience column,** describe where you feel it in your body, how tense or light it feels, and any reactions (tight chest, shallow breathing, warmth, restlessness).
- **In the Message / Meaning column,** explore what this emotion might be trying to communicate. For example: relief = "I survived an impossible moment," grief = "I loved deeply and feel loss," guilt = "I wished I could have done more."

TRACING THE TRUTH

MAPPING CONFLICTING EMOTIONS

Emotion **Body Sensations / Physical Experience** **Message / Meaning**

TRACING THE TRUTH

MAPPING CONFLICTING EMOTIONS

Emotion	Body Sensations / Physical Experience	Message / Meaning

WORRY WINDOW

Worries often hijack your mind, showing up at every unexpected moment. By giving them a dedicated "time slot," you reclaim control instead of letting them run your day. This practice teaches your nervous system that there's a safe space and a safe time to process, so you're not constantly reacting to every intrusive thought. During the window, you can gently evaluate what's actionable versus what you need to let go, building clarity and self-trust. Outside the window, a simple cue like "not now—later" helps you return to the present without guilt or shame. Over time, this simple structure reduces the intensity and frequency of anxious loops.

Park your worries: Write them down as they arise.

....

....

....

....

Set a 15-minute window: Choose a consistent time each day for processing.

....

Outside the window: Use a cue phrase like "not now—later" to return to your day.

Inside the window: Review the list. Solve what's actionable, accept what isn't, and release judgment.

Close the window: End with a grounding or soothing activity to signal completion.

GENTLE BREATH FOCUS

When anxiety spikes, the mind and body race together — thoughts accelerate, heart rate climbs, muscles tighten. Counting your breath gives both something steady to follow. By pairing inhale and exhale with numbers, you create a gentle anchor that slows the nervous system, refocuses attention, and interrupts spiraling thoughts. This isn't about perfection or achieving ten — it's about returning to the rhythm whenever distraction occurs. Even a few minutes daily strengthens your capacity to notice tension, settle your body, and move through anxious moments with less overwhelm.

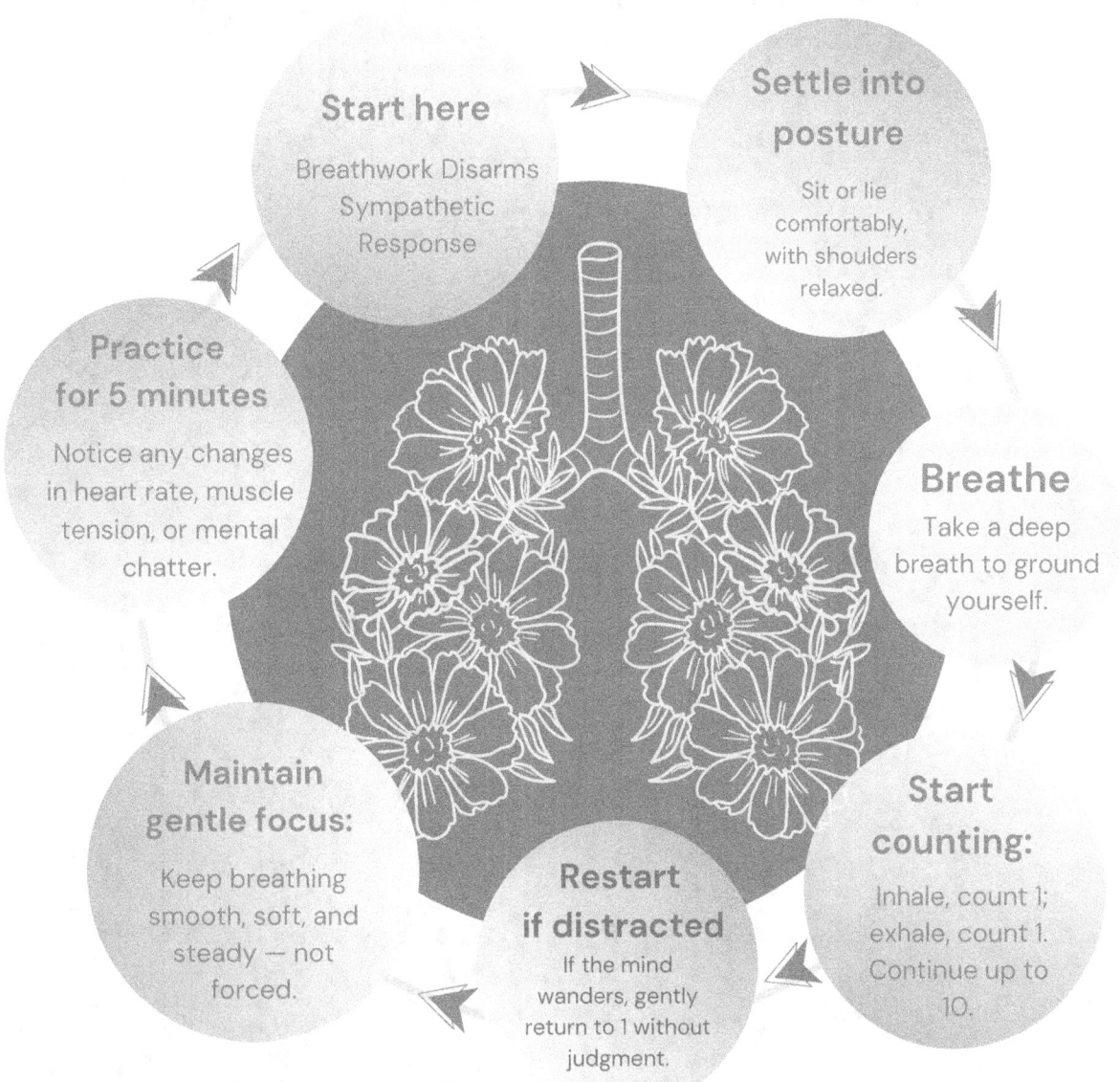

Start here
Breathwork Disarms Sympathetic Response

Settle into posture
Sit or lie comfortably, with shoulders relaxed.

Breathe
Take a deep breath to ground yourself.

Start counting:
Inhale, count 1; exhale, count 1. Continue up to 10.

Restart if distracted
If the mind wanders, gently return to 1 without judgment.

Maintain gentle focus:
Keep breathing smooth, soft, and steady — not forced.

Practice for 5 minutes
Notice any changes in heart rate, muscle tension, or mental chatter.

SECTION EIGHT

The Loneliness of Doing the Right Thing

You made the decision. Maybe alone. Maybe after begging for alternatives. Maybe after months or years of trying everything you could. And then — silence. Or worse, disbelief. Judgment. People saying, "I could never do that."

You're left sitting in a silence that feels like exile. Behavioral euthanasia is often invisible grief. It doesn't come with sympathy cards or understanding. It's not talked about over coffee or in support groups. You might find yourself pulling back from people you love — unsure if they'll understand, or terrified they'll say something that shatters you.

This kind of grief is lonely not just because you lost your pet — but because you lost the version of yourself who still believed others would stand beside you in this. In this section, we'll make room for the isolation. Not to collapse under it, but to name it. Because naming loneliness makes it less sharp. And being witnessed, even here, begins to stitch a little safety back into your world.

Making Sense Of It
The Solitude of Hard Decisions

Some of the heaviest grief is invisible. It comes from choices that are necessary, moral, and heartbreaking — like behavioral euthanasia. Anthropologists and grief researchers note that humans have evolved to rely on social mirrors: when our losses are acknowledged, validated, and held by community, our nervous systems can regulate and process pain. When those mirrors are absent, grief feels suspended, and the body reacts as if the threat is ongoing. Your heart races, your chest tightens, your mind replays every decision — all normal biological responses to extreme stress.

This loneliness is not a sign of weakness or failure. It's an adaptive response: you're navigating one of the few human experiences that most people cannot fully witness or understand. Studies on disenfranchised grief show that people in morally complex situations — making choices to protect, prevent suffering, or enforce boundaries — often experience prolonged grief and guilt precisely because the social world cannot hold their pain.

Many instinctively retreat from friends or family, downplay the loss, or avoid spaces where judgment feels imminent. That self-protection is intelligent: it preserves emotional energy while your nervous system recalibrates. Healing begins when you reclaim the story for yourself — naming your grief, validating your decisions, and witnessing your own courage. Even if no one else can see it, your choice was humane. Your grief is real. And your love — even in isolation — is undeniable.

Where did you expect support — and didn't receive it?

Name the people or spaces where you hoped for kindness. Let yourself acknowledge the absence, without minimizing your expectations.

Where did you expect support — and didn't receive it?

Have you told the full truth about what happened — and if not, why?

Explore what you've shared, withheld, or edited. Was it for safety? To protect others? To protect yourself from shame?

Have you told the full truth about what happened — and if not, why?

What responses from others have helped — even a little?

Name the words, gestures, or people who made you feel less alone. Honor them here, even if they were small.

What responses from others have helped — even a little?

What would it mean to stop explaining your decision?

What changes — in your self-perception, your grief, your power — if you no longer try to justify the unexplainable?

What would it mean to stop explaining your decision?

What parts of your grief feel safest in solitude? Which parts ache for companionship?

Grief doesn't always want company — but sometimes it does. Let yourself name where you long to be seen.

What parts of your grief feel safest in solitude? Which parts ache for companionship?

TRACING THE TRUTH

THE LETTER I NEEDED

Sometimes the people around us can't or won't give the support we need – and the grief feels heavier for it. This exercise lets you step into that missing kindness and hear the words you most needed. It creates a bridge between isolation and self-compassion, validating the truth of your experience.

Why it helps:
This exercise rewires your internal narrative. By giving voice to validation that may have been absent, you reduce shame, reconnect with your own compassion, and create a tangible anchor for healing.

Write a letter to yourself from the person you needed support from. It could be a friend, vet, family member, or an imagined person who says everything you needed to hear.
Begin with: "I want you to know I see the cost of what you did…"
Let the letter validate you, love you, and name your courage.
Read it aloud (or whisper it). Let your nervous system hear the words. Even if they didn't come in real life, this creates a bridge – a repair.
Keep the letter somewhere visible. Let this be your mirror when the world refuses to reflect the truth

TRACING THE TRUTH

THE LETTER I NEEDED

TRACING THE TRUTH

THE LETTER I NEEDED

TRACING THE TRUTH

THE LETTER I NEEDED

TRACING THE TRUTH

SOLITUDE OF YOUR CHOICES

Grieving a morally difficult loss can feel isolating. This exercise helps you name what you felt, why it mattered, and how your inner witness can honor it – giving voice to grief that has no external audience.

Why it helps:
By externalizing your choices and emotions, you give your nervous system permission to process the grief without judgment. You also reclaim your story from silence and validate your own courage, even in isolation.
Optional: Revisit the table later and add a fourth column: "How I Can Be Gentle With Myself Now" to track your healing over time.

Fill out the table on the next page.
- **In the first column**, write the specific choice or action that weighed heavily on you.
- **In the second column**, list all the emotions connected to that choice – even the conflicting ones.
- **In the third column**, honor what this moment says about your character, values, and humanity.

TRACING THE TRUTH

SOLITUDE OF YOUR CHOICES

| Choices That Hurt | The Emotions It Caused | Compassionate Reflection |

TRACING THE TRUTH

SOLITUDE OF YOUR CHOICES

Choices That Hurt

The Emotions It Caused

Compassionate Reflection

ACTION

LEAVES ON A STREAM

We often get stuck in our thoughts, treating them as commands or facts, which fuels stress and emotional overwhelm. Defusion teaches you to step back and see thoughts as just thoughts—mental events that come and go. By visualizing them on leaves drifting down a stream, you give your mind space to notice them without reacting. This practice reduces the pull of negative thinking, strengthens present-moment awareness, and improves emotional flexibility.

Sit quietly and settle. Take a few slow breaths, noticing your body and surroundings.

Visualize the stream. Picture a gentle stream flowing in front of you.

Place thoughts on leaves. Each time a thought appears, imagine putting it on a leaf floating by.

Label hooked moments. If you notice you're caught up in a thought, gently label it "thinking" and return it to the stream.

Continue for 5–10 minutes. Keep observing without judgment, letting each thought drift away.

ACTION

MOMENT-TO-MOMENT AWARENESS

Our minds are constantly busy—hearing, thinking, planning, feeling—and it's easy to get swept away in the stream of thoughts and sensations. This practice helps you step back and notice what's happening in the present without getting stuck. By softly labeling each experience, you create a gentle separation between yourself and the flood of mental activity. Even a short daily practice trains your attention, lowers emotional reactivity, and strengthens the ability to return to calm focus when life gets overwhelming.

Set a timer for 5 minutes so you can fully commit without checking the clock.

Sit comfortably and close your eyes if you like.

Notice experiences as they arise. Softly label them as: "hearing... thinking... planning... feeling..."

Return to your breath. After labeling, bring your attention back to your natural breathing.

Repeat gently. Whenever your mind wanders, notice it, label it, and return to the breath without judgment.

SECTION NINE

Regret, Rumination, and the Loop That Won't Let Go

Regret is a cruel visitor. It doesn't knock politely. It barges in at 2AM with its fists full of what-ifs and its mouth full of shame.

"Maybe I should have tried harder."
"What if I waited one more day?"
"What if I was wrong?"

Behavioral euthanasia is especially vulnerable to regret because there is no tidy ending. You didn't lose your pet to illness or old age. You made a call — a loving, impossible, trauma-soaked call — and now your brain won't let it settle.

This section is not about forcing closure. It's about offering your nervous system the safety it's craving. The loop persists not because you failed — but because your mind is trying to find a way back in time, to rescue both of you.

Making Sense Of It
Why Your Mind Won't Stop Turning It Over

Rumination is often misunderstood. We think it means weakness, obsession, or moral failure — but the truth is far more nuanced. From a neurobiological perspective, it's a survival mechanism. Your brain is wired to replay high-stakes, emotionally charged events, searching for a way to prevent harm, even when nothing could have changed the outcome.

After moral injury — like making a devastating choice for a pet's safety or well-being — the mind becomes especially insistent. It keeps turning the same question over and over: "Could I have done better? Did I fail?" This loop isn't proof of guilt; it's a signal that your nervous system is still integrating the experience, still trying to restore a sense of safety and coherence.

Trauma interrupts the natural closure of memory, leaving fragments of fear, grief, and responsibility spinning. When we meet rumination with judgment or self-criticism, we amplify shame and stall healing. But when we approach it with curiosity and compassion — observing the "what ifs" and "should haves" without trying to fix them — we soothe the parts of ourselves still trapped in the event.

Over time, this mindful attention builds internal trust: the part of you that endured, that loved, and that made the most humane choice begins to recognize its own wisdom. Rumination shifts from a prison to a teacher, guiding the nervous system toward integration, acceptance, and eventual peace.

What moment does your mind keep going back to — and what does it say when it gets there?

Name the specific memory that haunts you. What's the story your brain replays? Be honest, even if it's messy.

What moment does your mind keep going back to — and what does it say when it gets there?

If regret had a voice, what would it sound like? Who does it remind you of?

Explore the tone of your inner critic. Is it cruel? Helpless? Protective? Sometimes regret echoes an old wound.

If regret had a voice, what would it sound like? Who does it remind you of?

What do you think your brain is trying to protect you from by looping this story?

Rumination often serves a purpose — like trying to make sense of chaos, or preventing future harm. Get curious about its function.

What do you think your brain is trying to protect you from by looping this story?

Can you remember a time you did act with courage, even if the outcome still hurt?

Balance the picture. Let yourself recall a moment where you made a painful but loving choice. Let it stand beside the regret.

Can you remember a time you did act with courage, even if the outcome still hurt?

What would you say to a friend stuck in this same loop? Can you offer that to yourself, too?

Use your own wisdom. Practice giving yourself the grace you'd never withhold from someone else in your shoes.

What would you say to a friend stuck in this same loop? Can you offer that to yourself, too?

TRACING THE TRUTH

BREAKING THE LOOP

Trauma often traps us in a mental loop, replaying the moments, "what ifs," or regrets over and over. This isn't weakness — it's your nervous system trying to process an impossible situation. This exercise helps you externalize the loop, witness it without judgment, and gently guide your mind toward integration and self-compassion.

Why it helps:
Externalizing the loop removes it from your identity and reduces its emotional intensity. Speaking it aloud creates witness and validation. Bilateral tapping helps regulate the nervous system, and rewriting the ending introduces a compassionate, realistic narrative that allows your mind and body to release the stuck stress response. Over time, this strengthens internal trust and reduces the mental spinning of regret.

Externalize: Write or draw your loop — phrases, memories, or images that repeat. Arrows or circles are fine; messiness is welcome.
Speak It: Read the loop aloud. Treat it like a separate voice: "You keep showing me the last night. You want to go back."
Ground: Tap your hands gently on your thighs, alternating sides while repeating the loop once more. Remind your body: I am here. I am safe.
Rewrite the Ending: Add one sentence of truth and compassion: "And even so, I loved them. I stayed. I made the hardest choice a heart can make."

TRACING THE TRUTH

BREAKING THE LOOP

TRACING THE TRUTH

BREAKING THE LOOP

ACTION

FEEL IT, DON'T FEED IT

Neuroscience shows that most emotions, if left alone, rise, crest, and fall within about 90 seconds. What keeps us trapped is the story we add — the rumination, replaying, and self-criticism. The 90-Second Emotion Wave helps you move through the raw sensation without getting stuck in the mental loops that amplify pain. By anchoring your attention to your breath and gently offering your body comfort, you allow the emotion to pass through instead of drowning in it. This teaches you that emotions are temporary visitors, not permanent truths.

Set a timer for 90 seconds.

Notice the emotion rise. Imagine it as a wave building. Stay with the body sensations.

Anchor with breath. Breathe slowly, lengthening your exhale. Place a hand where the emotion feels strongest in your body.

Ride the crest. Let the feeling peak without pushing it away or fueling it.

Allow the fall. As the wave settles, ask yourself softly: "What do I need now?"

ACTION

KIND INTENTION SETTING

Intentions are like a quiet compass. They don't pressure you or set you up to "succeed" or "fail." They just give you something gentle to return to when the day gets noisy. Starting your morning with one small sentence helps you set the tone: maybe you want to be steadier, softer, braver. Ending the day with another sentence helps you notice where you actually showed up, without the self-punishment. It's less about performance and more about self-trust — proof that you can guide yourself kindly, one day at a time.

Morning: Write one line — "Today, I will show up with ___." (e.g., patience, presence, steadiness).

Carry it lightly: Let it sit in the back of your mind; check in when you feel pulled off course.

Evening: Write one line — "Today, I showed up with ___." Be honest, but kind.

Close the loop: Let the day go. Tomorrow is fresh.

SECTION TEN

Who Am I Now Without Them?

When your pet died, it wasn't just them that was lost. It was the way you woke up. The way your days had structure. The way your home felt alive. The little rituals. The language only the two of you understood.

But beyond all that, you also lost a version of you. The person who loved them, protected them, tried endlessly for them. The version of you who had a pet.

Now what's left feels blurry. Unanchored. You don't know who you are anymore. And the world moves on like nothing happened. That confusion — that aching emptiness where identity used to be — is a form of grief that often goes unnamed. But it matters.

You are still here. But you are not the same. And that disorientation? It's not weakness. It's what happens when love leaves a crater in the middle of your life. This chapter helps you begin to find your shape again — gently, piece by piece.

Making Sense Of It
When the Caretaker Self Fractures

Humans don't just form attachments to animals — we form identities through them. Caregiving creates structure, purpose, and meaning in our daily lives. From a psychological perspective, the act of caring for another sentient being activates reward and attachment circuits in the brain, particularly in the oxytocinergic and mesolimbic pathways. These systems reinforce feelings of competence, love, and purpose, linking identity directly to the role we inhabit. When that caregiving role ends abruptly, especially through morally and emotionally complex situations like behavioral euthanasia, it can produce what trauma researchers call a rupture in self-continuity: the sense that the "past self" and "present self" no longer recognize each other.

Anthropologically, humans have historically defined themselves through their relationships with dependent beings — children, kin, domesticated animals, and community members. In small-scale societies, the capacity to protect, feed, and advocate for those who cannot protect themselves was not optional; it was central to social cohesion and survival. Losing the ability to perform that role can trigger a profound existential disorientation because identity has always been interwoven with responsibility, caretaking, and moral agency.

Making Sense Of It
When the Caretaker Self Fractures

Neurologically, prolonged caregiving activates predictive and anticipatory networks: the brain learns to expect routines, safety threats, and emotional feedback loops. When the caregiver role ends suddenly, those networks remain active for weeks or months, leaving the nervous system in a state of unresolved expectation, often experienced as anxiety, emptiness, or dislocation. This isn't a flaw — it's the nervous system signaling that an integral part of your identity has been disrupted and requires reintegration.

Psychologically, this rupture often brings hyper-responsibility and rumination. You may replay choices, question competence, or feel fragmented, because identity itself has been tethered to the caregiving role. Recognizing this is critical: the disruption isn't evidence of weakness, guilt, or failure — it's a natural consequence of a complex neurobiological and social system suddenly altered. Healing emerges not by erasing the past, but by acknowledging the layers of attachment, care, and meaning that once defined you, and understanding that these layers remain part of your lived experience even after the role ends.

What roles did your pet give you?

Write freely: protector, nurse, comedian, parent, lifeline, home. Let yourself honor all the ways you were changed by loving them.

What roles did your pet give you?

What parts of yourself feel missing now?

Explore what you feel you lost — not just them, but the you who existed alongside them.

What parts of yourself feel missing now?

Who are you when no one needs you?

A painful question — but one worth asking. Let yourself explore this with softness, not pressure.

Who are you when no one needs you?

What remains unchanged about you?

Even in grief, some truths remain. What parts of you feel familiar, even now?

What remains unchanged about you?

If your pet could see you now, what would they still recognize?

Imagine their gaze on you. What would they still know? What would they still love?

If your pet could see you now, what would they still recognize?

TRACING THE TRUTH

RECONNECT WITH THE SELF YOU'VE LOST

After a traumatic loss, it's common to feel like a part of yourself has disappeared – the caregiver, protector, and companion you once were. This exercise helps you reconnect with that lost self, offering gentle acknowledgment, compassion, and presence. It's a small, deliberate way to let your grieving self be seen, held, and remembered.

Why it helps:
This simple, grounded practice reconnects you with the self that feels lost. It signals to your nervous system that it is safe to feel, acknowledge, and integrate your grief. Over time, it strengthens internal validation and begins to repair the identity fracture left by your loss.

Settle into stillness: Find a quiet spot where you won't be disturbed. Take a few slow breaths and allow yourself to arrive fully in the moment.
Meet your eyes: Sit in front of a mirror and look into your own eyes. Let yourself simply witness, without judgment or expectation.
Speak to the grieving self: Offer words of compassion to the part of you that's hurting:
- "You are not broken; you are evolving."
- "You were a devoted [pet] parent; that love mattered."
- "It's okay if you don't recognize yourself right now."

Seal it with touch: Place your hand on your chest or cheek and whisper: "I'm still here." Let your body feel the truth of your presence.

ACTION

THE BREATH SQUARE

When anxiety floods you, your brain hijacks the moment with "what ifs." This tool cuts through spirals by anchoring you in your body's real-time experience. It reactivates the sensory pathways, pulling you out of mental overdrive and into the safety of the present moment. Instead of fighting thoughts, you drop into your senses — a place your nervous system recognizes as grounding.

Inhale for 4 as you trace the first side.

Hold for 4 as you trace the next side.

Exhale for 4 as you trace the third side.

Hold for 4 as you complete the square.

Repeat this cycle 3–5 times. Keep your pace steady — not too fast, not too slow. Imagine you're sketching calm into the air with each breath.

ACTION

ANCHOR OBJECT

When your thoughts spiral, your body needs a safe place to land. Touching and describing an object interrupts the overwhelm and pulls your attention into the present moment. The sensory detail gives your nervous system something concrete to hold onto, which helps quiet racing thoughts. This isn't about distracting yourself — it's about anchoring, reminding your brain: I'm here, I'm safe, I'm grounded.

Pick up a small object — maybe a coin, a stone, or something you often carry. Hold it gently in your hand and really notice it. Ask yourself: What's the temperature? Is it cool or warm? What texture do I feel — smooth, rough, bumpy? How heavy or light does it seem?

Slowly describe these details to yourself, either silently or out loud, as if you're pointing them out to a curious friend. Stay with it for 2–3 minutes, letting your mind settle on the simple, steady presence of the object.

ACTION

SAFE SPACE SCAN

When our mind races with worry or panic, it often ignores the present and imagines danger that isn't real. This simple room scan draws your attention to concrete details, giving your nervous system proof of safety. Naming what's around you slows your thoughts, helps you orient to the present, and reminds your body: I'm here, I'm safe enough, and I can move from here with calm.

① Take a moment to pause wherever you are.

② Slowly look around the room and notice details:

- **The colors** on walls, furniture, or objects.
- **The corners** and edges of the space.
- **Light sources** — windows, lamps, or overhead lights.
- **Exits or places you could leave** if you needed to.

③ As you do this, repeat to yourself: "I am safe enough right now." Let your attention linger on the room's details for 1–2 minutes, noticing how your body responds.

SECTION ELEVEN

Rebuilding Trust

After behavioral euthanasia, trust can feel like shattered glass.
You might not trust the world — a world that didn't help you enough, didn't understand, didn't save your pet. You might not trust other people — those who judged, stayed silent, or walked away. You might not trust yourself — the version of you who tried everything and still couldn't fix it.

That fracture runs deep. And grief wrapped in shame can harden into a belief: I should've done better. I shouldn't try again. This chapter isn't about forcing optimism. It's about giving you permission to gently reenter life — on your terms, at your pace. It's about noticing the parts of you that still believe in connection... even after everything.

Because trust isn't built in grand declarations. It's built in small, quiet yeses — to hope, to truth, to softness, to life again.

Making Sense Of It
Rebuilding Trust After Trauma

Trust is not merely an intellectual concept; it is a felt experience, encoded in the nervous system. Trauma, especially morally wrenching events like behavioral euthanasia, rewires both mind and body. Psychologically, this manifests as hypervigilance, intrusive thoughts, and heightened startle responses — the brain's attempt to prevent future harm. Anthropologically, humans are wired to survive through social attunement: we rely on cues from others to gauge safety. When a loss occurs in isolation, or in the shadow of judgment and guilt, the nervous system interprets social cues as potential threats, and vulnerability becomes biologically unsafe.

Cognitive neuroscience shows that moral injury — acting against deeply held values, even out of necessity — amplifies this disruption. The prefrontal cortex, responsible for reasoning, struggles to regulate the amygdala's threat signals. The result: a persistent somatic anxiety, a body that remembers what the mind wants to forget. Rebuilding trust, then, is an embodied process. Micro-repair — consistent, gentle signals of safety — is essential. A friend's unjudging presence, mindful breathwork, or the simple act of noticing your heartbeat conveys to your nervous system: you are not in danger. Over time, these repeated, small acts recalibrate threat responses, allowing the body to feel connection without fear, and hope without betrayal.

Healing trust after trauma is not fast, linear, or purely mental. It is a rewiring of survival itself — a testament to human resilience and our species' capacity to recover intimacy, care, and compassion, even after profound loss.

What parts of the world do you feel you can't trust anymore?

Be honest — institutions, people, social groups, even your own instincts. Let the page hold it.

What parts of the world do you feel you can't trust anymore?

What was taken from you that made it harder to trust?

Name the specific losses — emotional, relational, spiritual. Acknowledge the rupture.

What was taken from you that made it harder to trust?

Who (if anyone) helped restore even a little trust during this time?

Even if it was just a kind word, an online post, or a moment of grace. Let yourself remember it.

Who (if anyone) helped restore even a little trust during this time?

What would it feel like to trust yourself again?

Describe it in detail — physically, emotionally, spiritually. Not what you should feel, but what it might feel like.

What would it feel like to trust yourself again?

If you could trust life just 5% more, what would you try?

Not a full leap — just a toe in the water. Let yourself explore this gently.

If you could trust life just 5% more, what would you try?

How has this grief made you more trustworthy to others?

Sometimes, the brokenhearted become the safest place for others. Could that be true of you?

How has this grief made you more trustworthy to others?

TRACING THE TRUTH

LETTER TO YOUR FUTURE SELF

Trust isn't rebuilt overnight. Your nervous system holds memories of fear, guilt, and moral injury long after the event has passed. Writing a letter to your future self is a powerful way to anchor safety, compassion, and reassurance into your body and mind. This exercise lets your present self speak with the wisdom and care your future self will need — it's a micro-repair practice for nervous-system healing.

Why it helps:
This exercise helps your brain and body learn that vulnerability is safe, grief and relief can coexist, and trust can be rebuilt over time.

Address Your Future Self: Start with: "Dear Future Me, learning to trust again…"
Name What You Feel Now: Briefly write your fear, tension, or grief — be honest.
Offer Compassion and Reassurance: Remind your future self: vulnerability is safe, relief doesn't erase love, and you survived a hard, morally complex choice.
Visualize Safety and Growth: Include one line imagining your future self calm, soft, and at ease.
Close with Love: Sign with warmth: "I see you. I honor you. You are safe to trust again."
Keep or Seal: Place the letter somewhere meaningful — revisit when your nervous system feels tense.

TRACING THE TRUTH

THE TRUTH YOU WEREN'T ALLOWED TO TELL

TRACING THE TRUTH

THE TRUTH YOU WEREN'T ALLOWED TO TELL

TRACING THE TRUTH

THE TRUTH YOU WEREN'T ALLOWED TO TELL

TRACING THE TRUTH

THE TRUTH YOU WEREN'T ALLOWED TO TELL

NERVOUS SYSTEM RESET

Sometimes your body gets stuck in high alert—heart racing, muscles tight, mind spiraling—and it's hard to think or respond clearly. TIP Skills target the physiology directly, calming your nervous system so your emotions have space to settle. Using temperature, movement, and breathing strategically helps you interrupt the stress response, release adrenaline, and regain a sense of control. This isn't about ignoring feelings—it's about resetting your body so you can respond thoughtfully instead of reacting out of overwhelm.

  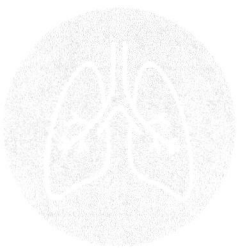 

T = TEMPERATURE

Splash cool water on your face or neck, or use a cold pack. This signals your body that it's safe to downshift.

I = INTENSE EXERCISE

Create several posts of the same type at once, schedule them using an app, and upload them so they are available at the right time

P = PACED BREATHING

You can save time by copying and pasting the CTA into your posts instead of writing it out again every time

P = PROGRESSIVE MUSCLE RELAXATION

Create some posts with a frame around your branding image.
You can reuse the same image after at least 9 posts but change the brand colour for a different look

FOUNDATIONS OF CALM

Our bodies and minds are deeply connected—when physical needs are neglected, emotions intensify and coping becomes harder. PLEASE encourages you to take care of your body in simple, practical ways that support emotional stability: eating regularly, sleeping well, moving your body, and avoiding substances that amplify stress or mood swings. Focusing on one small, achievable upgrade at a time helps you build sustainable habits without overwhelm. These micro-choices add up, giving your nervous system a solid foundation so your emotions and decisions feel clearer and calmer.

① **Pick one small upgrade today.** Example: add one glass of water, go for a 10-minute walk, or set a 15-minute wind-down before bed.

② **Notice the impact.** Record any shifts in mood, energy, or clarity.

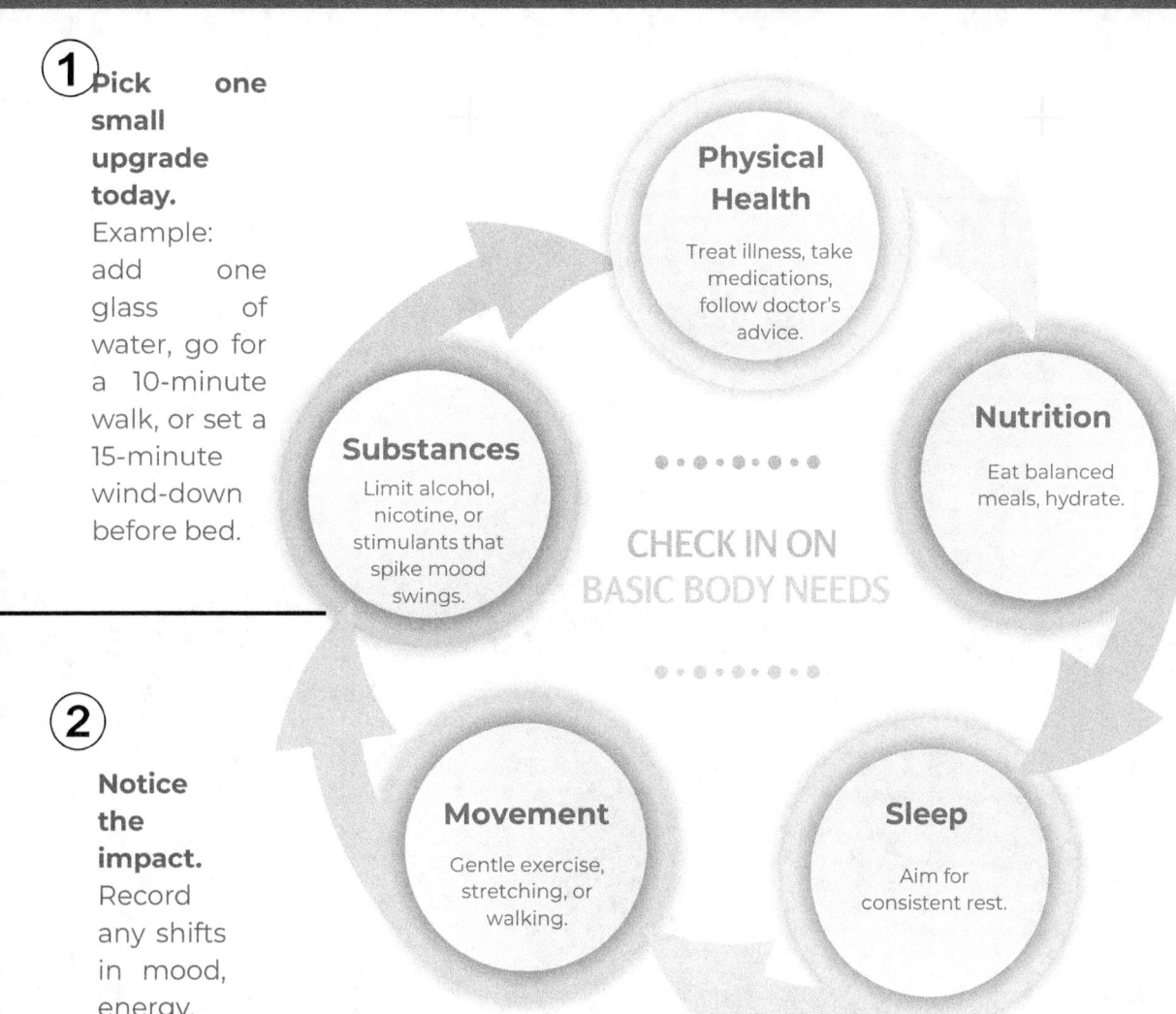

CHECK IN ON BASIC BODY NEEDS

- **Physical Health** — Treat illness, take medications, follow doctor's advice.
- **Nutrition** — Eat balanced meals, hydrate.
- **Sleep** — Aim for consistent rest.
- **Movement** — Gentle exercise, stretching, or walking.
- **Substances** — Limit alcohol, nicotine, or stimulants that spike mood swings.

STONEWELL HEALING PRESS

ASSESSMENT

HOW FAR I'VE COME

You've done the work — now let's see where you're at. Take a moment to rate these statements again with honesty and self-compassion. Notice what's shifted, what still feels raw, and what that means for your next steps.

1-10

1. How aware are you of your feelings about your loss, and how easily can you name them without judgment or suppression?

2. To what extent are you able to treat yourself with understanding and kindness instead of guilt, shame, or self-recrimination?

3. How comfortable are you recognizing that you can feel grief, relief, love, and even conflicting emotions all at the same time?

4. How capable are you of honoring and validating your grief, even when others don't understand, minimize, or dismiss it?

5. To what degree do you trust that your past choices — even painful, morally complex ones — were the most compassionate and responsible you could make?

6. How attuned are you to your body's signals of stress, grief, or relief, and how effectively can you soothe and ground yourself when triggered?

7. How able are you to integrate difficult, morally charged experiences without feeling permanently "damaged" or guilty?

8. How fully can you hold your story — the hopes, the grief, the love, and the limits — as your own, without erasing or minimizing any part of it?

Mindset & Identity Shift Reflection

Healing changes the way you see yourself. You might notice you're less reactive in certain moments, more confident speaking up, or simply softer with yourself. This page is about spotting those shifts — the ones that show you're not the same person who started this journey.

In what ways do I see myself differently than when I started?

What beliefs about myself or others are shifting?

How has my sense of hope, strength, or trust evolved?

MOVING FORWARD

ACTION PLAN

This is your personalized roadmap for continuing growth beyond this workbook. Use this space to clarify which skills you'll keep practicing, how you'll notice early warning signs, and what concrete steps you'll take to support yourself. Remember, transformation happens one intentional step at a time.

Skills I will keep practicing regularly	

Early warning signs or triggers I'll watch for:	

When I notice these signs, here's what I will do:	

MOVING FORWARD

ACTION PLAN

This is your personalized roadmap for continuing growth beyond this workbook. Use this space to clarify which skills you'll keep practicing, how you'll notice early warning signs, and what concrete steps you'll take to support yourself. Remember, transformation happens one intentional step at a time.

Ways I can check in with myself to monitor progress (daily, weekly, monthly):	
People or supports I will reach out to if I need encouragement or accountability:	
One commitment I'm making to myself right now:	

RESOURCE LIST

The resources listed here are shared for informational purposes only. While they provide valuable support and tools for mental health, I am not endorsing or guaranteeing the quality, effectiveness, or availability of their services. It's important to explore these options and verify the details directly on their websites to ensure they align with your personal needs.

National Alliance on Mental Illness

www.nami.org
Offers free mental health education, peer support, and a 24/7 helpline.

Insight Timer

www.insighttimer.com
A free meditation app with thousands of guided meditations, music, and talks on mental well-being

MuchLoved GriefChat

www.parentingformentalhealth.com
Provides a free online counselling service for bereaved individuals seeking support outside their immediate circle.

Crisis Text Line

www.crisistextline.org
Offers free, 24/7 text-based support for mental health crises

7 Cups

www.7cups.com
Offers free, anonymous online chat with trained volunteers, as well as paid therapy with licensed professionals.

There's a kind of grief that doesn't get spoken about. Not because it isn't real — but because it makes people uncomfortable. Behavioral euthanasia is like that. It lives in a silence most people don't know how to meet. Maybe your friends didn't say much. Maybe they tried to reassure you, or maybe they just changed the subject. But they didn't really get it. How could they? They didn't see what you saw. They didn't live through the fear, the hypervigilance, the hundreds of tiny choices you had to make to keep everyone safe. They didn't see you trying. Again and again. Hoping. Adjusting. They didn't see what it cost you — to love someone who was suffering and reactive and misunderstood. And they didn't see what it cost to let them go.

So now here you are. Alone in a grief that most people wouldn't even call grief. You made the right choice. And it still hurts like hell. Because it didn't feel like a choice. Because you loved them. There might not be closure. The world will move on — and most people won't remember. But you will. You'll remember everything. The way they looked at you when no one else was around. The good days, the impossibly hard ones. The weight of the decision.

And maybe the most honest thing to do now is to carry that love quietly. To not force it to become anything other than what it is — grief. Loss. The end of a story that never got to finish.

What you gave was enough. What you did was enough. Even if it broke your heart.

M. Tourangeau
Stonewell Healing Press

www.ingramcontent.com/pod-product-compliance
Lightning Source LLC
Chambersburg PA
CBHW080408230426
43662CB00016B/2352